Don’t Blame [illegible]ks

Five Leaves Bookshop Occasional Papers

* **The Current Status of Jerusalem** by Edward Said
978-1-910170-09-0, 32 pages, £4

* **Doctor Who and the Communist: Malcolm Hulke and his career in television** by Michael Herbert
978-1-910170-08-3, 32 pages, £4

Strengthening Democracy in Post-conflict Northern Ireland by Maria Power
978-1-910170-16-8, 32 pages, £4

Anarchy 38: Nottingham by Freedom Press
978-1-910170-18-2, 32 pages, £4

* **How We Live and How We Might Live** by William Morris
978-1-910170-26-7, 28 pages, £4

Harper Lee and the American South by Katie Hamilton
978-1-910170-27-4, 28 pages, £4

That Precious Strand of Jewishness that Challenges Authority by Leon Rosselson
978-1-910170-33-5, 28 pages, £4

* **Mad John's Walk** by John Gallas
978-1-910170-41-0, 16 pages, £3

Street Haunting by Virginia Woolf & **Bulwell** by Stanley Middleton
978-1-910170-42-7, 24 pages, £4

The Mask of Anarchy by Percy Bysshe Shelley
978-1-910170-48-9, 24 pages, £4

The Fear of Being Seen as White Losers by David Jackson
978-1-910170-54-0, 48 pages, £6

Byron Speaks Up for the Luddites by Lord Byron
978-1-910170-59-5, 24 pages, £4

Two Short Stories by DH Lawrence
978-1-910170-92-2, 32 pages, £4

500 Years of Struggle – A People's History of Nottingham by the Nottingham Communist Party (1949)
978-1-910170-76-2, 24 pages, £4

The Long Piece by Alan Sillitoe
978-1-910170-93-9, 48 pages, £6

Feminism Before the First Wave by Zoë Fairbairns
978-1-910170-94-6, 20 pages, £4

Available from Five Leaves or from other bookshops worldwide
(except papers marked * which are not currently available).
All prices include UK postage if ordered direct from Five Leaves Bookshop.

www.fiveleavesbookshop.co.uk

Don't Blame the Blacks

George Powe

Introduction by Panya Banjoko

with 'Island Screams'

by Cara Thompson

Five Leaves Bookshop Occasional Papers

Don't Blame the Blacks
George Powe

First published in 1956

This edition published in 2022
by Five Leaves Bookshop
14a Long Row, Nottingham NG1 2DH
www.fiveleavesbookshop.co.uk

Five Leaves Bookshop Occasional Paper 17
ISBN: 978-1-910170-98-4

Designed and typeset by Five Leaves Bookshop

Printed in Great Britain

Introduction

Panya Banjoko

George Powe's *Don't Blame the Blacks* (1956): an activist force behind the writing of political literature in Nottingham.

Don't Blame the Blacks is the earliest example of post-war political literature that concentrates on race inequalities in Nottingham, and it marks the beginning of a rich Black literary history in the city. Written using the language of the time, when the antiquated and now offensive term 'coloured' was employed as a race descriptor, it accentuates how times have changed and shifted since the 1950s. *Don't Blame the Blacks* is a distillation of multiple forms of discontent that preceded the 1958 Nottingham 'race riots', including everyday racial violence, myriad issues with substandard housing, a subpar education for Black children, low employment prospects, and tensions with those white trade unionists who resisted the employment of Black workers. Overall, the hostile environment equated to a 'colour bar' which (Oswald) George Powe (1926-2013) cited as a 'main weapon' used to divide the city's communities.[1] Institutional

[1] George Powe, *Don't Blame the Blacks* (Nottingham: Afro-West Indian Union, 1956, p. 8, Box 11, Folder 2, NBA.

hesitancy was grounded in the denial that a colour bar existed, and activists began to look beyond the city, securing allegiances with Black groups nationally as Parliament debated limiting the number of colonial migrants allowed into Britain.

Don't Blame the Blacks spoke specifically to the problems reported by Caribbean migrants who journeyed to Nottingham with high expectations on arrival. While many migrants from the Caribbean had experience of dealing with prejudices based on pigmentocracy, they were not prepared for the racism which collectively regraded them 'monolithically as "coloureds", "West Indians", "Blacks", "immigrants", and even "wogs"', with no reference even to class.[2] As Winston James and Clive Harris distil

succinctly, a new collective activist identity was fused 'in which race [had] a comparatively low salience to one in which social relations [were] deeply permeated by the idea of race and the phenomenon of racism'.[3] Pioneers who were ex-service personnel, as Powe was, anticipated a warm welcome for having proved themselves loyal. They were unprepared for the machinations of the 'dehumanising process' that Robert N. Murray described whilst documenting the experiences of World War II ex-service personnel in Nottingham. Having been

2 Winston James and Clive Harris, *Inside Babylon: The Caribbean Diaspora in Britain* (London: Verso, 1993), p. 239.

3 James and Harris, *Inside Babylon: The Caribbean Diaspora in Britain*, p. 254.

'constrained by the RAF discipline, by King's Rules and Air Council's regulations and last, but not least, by the Colonial Office', migrants discovered that 'with this protection gone, [they] were "thrown to the wolves".'[4] Ex-service personnel would prove to be a vocal and politicised presence in the city from 1946 and they were instrumental in delivering social justice work after learning first-hand that a racially tolerant and progressive Britain was a myth.[5] Powe cited the 'colour bar' as a 'main weapon' used by the ruling class to divide Black and minority ethnic orders from whites and, in his formulation, 'race' was being used as a diversionary tactic and class was the base of the city's inequalities.

He summed up the most divisive leaders in the white community as 'a set of crackpots trying to form a Ku Klux Klan organisation in Britain' and a 'ruling class' in Nottingham 'preaching racial propaganda to white workers [while] at the same time whispering into the [Black] workers' ears that [...] the white workers are against them'.[6] It is possible that the critique of the social climate in Nottingham contained in *Don't Blame the Blacks* was also directed at members

[4] Robert N. Murray, *Lest We Forget: The Experiences of World War II Westindian Ex-Service Personnel* (Nottingham: Nottinghamshire Westindian Combined Ex-services Association, 1996), p. 132.

[5] Marc Matera studies this phenomenon in *Black London: The Imperial Metropolis and Decolonization in the Twentieth Century* (Oakland, CA: University of California Press, 2015).

[6] Powe, *Don't Blame the Blacks*, p. 6.

of the Commonwealth Consultative Committee for the Welfare of Coloured People (CCCWCP), established in 1954 to deal with the welfare issues of the West Indian pioneers. Powe would call its members' behaviour 'divisive' after the 1958 'riots' in Nottingham and, as Daniel Lawrence discovered, 'even representatives of the more moderate [Black] organisations criticised the Committee'.[7] In 1970, Ira Katznelson would allege that the CCCWCP tried 'to replace some of the Europeans with colonial stooges' but that this did not change 'the basic character of the Committee whose purpose [was] to confuse [Black] people'.[8]

The publication of Powe's pamphlet laid bare the impetus behind his community activism. It was broad in terms of the number and range of organisations he founded—he was involved in most of Nottingham's Black community groups and organisations—and longitudinal in that he devoted decades of his life to Black community development in the city. He founded the Sugar Cane Club in 1967, Solidarity for Protection against

---

[7] Daniel Lawrence, *Black Migrants: White Natives: A Study of Race Relations in Nottingham* (Cambridge: Cambridge University Press, 1974), p. 178.

[8] Ira Katznelson 'The Politics of Racial Buffering in Nottingham, 1954-1968', *Race & Class* 11:4 (1970). Powe led a campaign to abolish the post Eric Irons held as Special Officer over a period of at least five months from December 6, 1964 to May 23, 1965. The campaign highlighted the role of the Committee in creating divisions by using Irons as a buffer between the Committee and the Black community and the fissures this caused among the pioneers. It marked a political divide between how Irons worked towards social justice and how Powe conducted activist affairs. Irons worked within the institutions that existed and within the parameters the Committee set out. Powe was more radical in determining a course of action and much more vocal in protest; for example, in relation to the racial disturbances in 1958. It has been said that Powe was at the heart of the riots, while Irons is notably known for helping Nottingham City Council address the problems following the racial disturbances.

Deprivation and Exploitation (SPADE) in 1968, and the Black People's Freedom Movement (BPFM) in 1971. He was a founder member of the African Caribbean National Artistic Centre (ACNA) in 1971 (pictured above), and of the Joint Indian Pakistani African Caribbean Centre (JIPAC) in the 1980s. He was a leading figure in city campaigns, notably the Anti-Colour Bar Campaign and the Campaign to Abolish Special Officers for Coloured People in 1964. He provided valuable advice to Black men and women on their immigration rights. As an educator, he spent several years teaching mathematics in secondary schools.

In 1963, Powe was elected as a Labour Councillor to represent Sawley Ward on the Long Eaton Urban District Council, seven miles southwest of Nottingham, which made international news, appearing in publications in the USA.[9] This provided an opportunity for him to build on diasporic and transatlantic connections. Powe also began working closely with Nottingham Black Archive in 2011, making significant donations to the

[9] Charles L. Sanders, 'Race Problems in Great Britain: Bias forces 'coloreds' to band together for survival as in U.S.' *Ebony Magazine* (November 1965), pp. 146-148, 150, 152-159.

archive, and remained heavily involved in Nottingham's Black community until his death in 2013.

Don't Blame the Blacks was published under the auspices of the African West Indian Union (AWIU) where Powe served as secretary. It is the antecedent document heralding a series of burgeoning Black political organisations that would bind migrants from the Caribbean, Africa, and South Asia together in social protest, initiated when Powe's AWIU joined forces with the Indian Workers Association (IWA) as the Afro-Asian West Indian Union (AAWIU) in around 1961. 10,000 copies of his pamphlet were distributed and the London representative for the AWIU reported that it was also shared widely through its London branch. In Nottingham, it went on sale at Jordan's International Bookshop on Dane Street in St Ann's. Orders also came in from Africa and America.[10] Powe was at the forefront of AWIU,

[10] Oswald George Powe, 'Intergenerational Project', interviewed by Panya Banjoko, August 2011; Sylvia Riley, *Winter at the Bookshop: Politics and Poverty in St Ann's in the 1960s* (Nottingham: Five Leaves Publications, 2019), p. 95.

positioning it as an organisation to be consulted over instances of discrimination and saw part of its remit as 'developing a mutual understanding among all races'.[11] This was at the forefront of his mind when writing *Don't Blame the Blacks*, in which he rallied white comrades to the anti-racist cause, inviting a white trade unionist, John James (Jack) Charlesworth (1900–1993) to write a Foreword. Charlesworth was a trade union leader from Basford, Nottingham. He was a member of the Communist Party of Great Britain in 1930, president of the Trades' Council in 1941 and 1942 and assistant secretary from 1943. During his time as an elected secretary of the Nottingham and District Trades Council (from 1950), Charlesworth focused on industrial affairs, peace, and opposition to racism.

In his pamphlet Powe made his target audience explicit—trade unionists, socialists and the working class more broadly—and crafted an argument for capitalism and class as root causes of inequality before focusing on 'race' and racism. In this sense, his views preceded A. Sivanandan's concerted activist writing which refused to divide race from class, epitomised in 'From Resistance to Rebellion' (1981) in *Race & Class*.[12] Powe should be read as someone who advanced ideas that Sivanandan, Stuart Hall, and Paul Gilroy would explore in much greater detail in later decades.

In 1956, Powe predicted that, if left unchecked, racism in Nottingham would 'very rapidly' develop into 'a burning issue'. In 1958, Powe witnessed white-instigated 'race riots' in Nottingham.

[11] Records of AWIU's work include evidence of public meetings, of working collectively with the London branch of AWIU, advocacy, and distribution of race relations material. From 1958 through 1961, the AWIU evolved into the Afro-Asian West Indian Union (AAWIU) signalling a wider recognition of other oppressed groups active in the city.

[12] A. Sivanandan, 'From Resistance to Rebellion: Asian and Afro-Caribbean Struggles in Britain,' *Race & Class* XXIII: 2 (1981/2): pp. 11-152.

News reporters who descended watched 'thousands' of white people on the city's streets shouting, 'Let's get the blacks', but only twenty-four white people were arrested.[13] This was the second significant racial disturbance he experienced first-hand in the UK. He was in Birmingham in 1949 when racist energies were focused on Black former servicemen, notably at the Causeway Green army hostel which was the fulcrum of racist attack. This hostel is recorded as Powe's address on the certificate of his first marriage on September 13, 1949.[14]

It is telling that in 1956, in his pamphlet's title, Powe elected to use 'Black'. It was not the nomenclature that immigrant pioneers typically used to describe themselves: 'West Indian' or 'coloured' proliferated as common terms used by Blacks as well as whites. That he chose 'Black' is a political statement. A decade before 'Black Power' was promulgated as a rallying cry in 1966, Powe appropriated 'Black' for his political purposes because in 1950s' Britain it was more usually scrawled in graffiti as an insult or used in ubiquitous signs designed to dissuade Black people from seeking accommodation or applying for job vacancies, signs like those Powe highlighted in his pamphlet that were demanding citizens to 'Keep Britain White'. Powe wrote unequivocally against that imperative and outlined how 'deplorable conditions are not caused by accident, but deliberately created by the ruling class,

---

[13] Peter Fryer was among the reporters and describes this in *Staying Power: The History of Black People in Britain* (London: Pluto, 1984), p. 377.

[14] Powe's wedding certificate, Box 29, Folder 1, NBA. Powe resided in Birmingham until January 10, 1950, when he moved to 88 Jubilee Street, West Bromwich before settling in Nottinghamshire. See also, Kevin Searle, 'Mixing of the Unmixables: The 1949 Causeway Green "riots" in Birmingham', *Race & Class*, 54. 3 (2013), pp. 44-64 and Searle's essay 'Before Notting Hill: The Causeway Green "rioting" of 1949' *Black British History: New Perspectives* ed. Hakim Adi (London: Zed Books, 2019), pp. 90-105.

George Powe with Jill Westby

in order [to maintain a] system of exploitation'.[15] Read back through the lens of his later activism, I would suggest that in *Don't Blame the Blacks* Powe was also looking beyond Nottingham to Africa and America and towards an inclusive Pan-Africanism that drew on the intellectual work of other, and better-known, Caribbean-born activists, like George Padmore and C.L.R James.[16]

In this febrile context, the imperative 'Don't Blame the Blacks' was not only urgent but also courageous, especially as an intervention that refuted the so-called 'colour-blind' approach endorsed by Mr W.F. Laird, Chairman, and founder of the NCCWCP, which believed that whites in Nottingham could 'be congratulated that their fellow British citizens are settling down well and are rapidly winning the

[15] Powe, *Don't Blame the Blacks*, p. 2.

[16] George Padmore's *Pan-Africanism or Communism? The Coming Struggle for Africa* was published in 1956. He arrived in the UK in 1932, committed himself to the freedom struggle and acted as primary organiser of the Pan-African Congress held in Manchester in 1945. C.L.R. James reflected on Pan-Africanism and his relationship with Padmore in 'Reflections on Pan-Africanism' in 1973 at <https://www.marxists.org/archive/james-clr/works/1973/panafricanism.htm> [accessed 2 June 2022].

reputation of being hard workers'.[17] While Powe began the discourse on 'race' in Nottingham, others would continue to pull at this thread in the 1970s and the 1980s in an attempt to unravel the discriminatory practices of Nottingham's host community.

Inspired by the life of Powe and wanting to ensure this history remained current and accessible to younger generations when invited to contribute to the *Dawn of the Unread* series in 2016 I chose Powe and George Africanus as the protagonists for a digital graphic novel. I wanted to ensure that Powe's contribution to politics and literature was documented along with the community of Black writers in Nottingham.[18]

In June 2021, on the 73rd anniversary of the arrival of Empire Windrush, Powe was recognised again through the Nottingham Black Archive Exhibition at Nottingham Castle Museum and Gallery, entitled 'Don't Blame the Blacks'. The exhibition highlighted Powe's work in mobilising and motivating the local community to fight workplace discrimination and bring about change at Raleigh Industries, one of the largest employers of Black people in post-war Nottingham.[19] It provided an insight into the role Black communities in Nottingham played in combatting racism during, and since, the 1950s. It featured impressive photography by Vanley Burke of former Raleigh employees, video work by Keith Piper, and artefacts from the Nottingham Black Archive collection. Sadly, the racism that Powe

[17] Mr W.F. Laird, 'Letters from Readers: Homes Sought for City Coloured Immigrants', *Nottingham Evening Post*, 4 March 1955, Nottinghamshire Archives Black History Cuttings, Surrogate File, p. 23.

[18] Banjoko, Panya, 'Powe Meets Africanus', *Dawn of the Unread*, ed. James Walker, (Nottingham: Spokesman Books, 2016) Powe Meets Africanus can be found here, <http://www.dawnoftheunread.com/issue-16-01.html> [accessed 19 June 2022].

[19] www.whenweworkedatraleigh.wordpress.com

had fought against marred the exhibition when Nottingham Castle Trust was propelled into the spotlight for poor handling of a racist incident on site. Failure by the Castle to respond in accordance with their safeguarding policy led to an independent report being commissioned which highlighted significant failings by the Castle's Trust to safeguard minors, the issuing of 'formal advice and guidance' by the Charity Commission, and a call for a new ethnically representative governing board at the Castle by over 700 concerned citizens. I am sure if he were alive, Powe would have joined in the protest. Through his activism Powe, and his donations to Nottingham Black Archive, the history of Black political mobilisation in Nottingham can begin to be mapped, acknowledged and, I hope, it will provide a lasting legacy for future generations. *Don't Blame the Blacks* is a foundational cornerstone in this endeavour.

Don't Blame the Blacks

FOREWORD

This pamphlet is designed to present the facts as to why the coloured worker seeks his livelihood in our midst; not an easy task to undertake and yet its author has accomplished much more! It is no apology for his coming; set out in this brief compass, in a readable and commonsense way, is the story of a section of the world's workers that all trade unionists are recommended to study.

It is not to be expected that every reader will be in complete agreement with all its contents but insofar as it provokes thought amongst workers to counter, what is, unfortunately, too often a blind and unreasoned prejudice against our coloured friends, it will have served its purpose.

The sponsors, the Afro-West Indian Union, are to be congratulated on their effort to unite workers in defence of, and in the furtherance of, industrial conditions.

JACK CHARLESWORTH
Secretary
Nottingham and District Trades Council

INTRODUCTION

Every day we read reports in the newspapers of redundancy and short-time working being introduced in industry all over Britain.

At the same time another development is taking place in Birmingham, London and other towns. The letters K.B.W. (Keep Britain White) appeared white-washed on walls, and a well-known M.P. has had swastikas and similar slogans painted on his house as a punishment for introducing a Bill in the House of Commons to make colour discrimination illegal in public places. There are also reports of a set of crackpots trying to form a Ku Klux Klan organisation in Britain.

Articles have appeared in the sensational press with such titles as 'Stop them now; the coloured invasion has gone too far,' 'Do we owe them a living?' Some responsible officials are crying out that something must be done to control the influx of immigrants without even uttering a word what should be done to cure THE SOCIAL AND ECONOMIC ILLS WHICH DRIVE THE COLOURED IMMIGRANTS TO EMIGRATE.

Without clarity these reports could be the elements of a very explosive situation which could develop overnight. The colour problem in Britain may not appear to be important now, but very rapidly it could develop into a burning issue, into a situation fraught with dangers for both coloured and white workers.

In this pamphlet we aim to show the English worker why this question is so important to him and that it is not just a coloured workers' affair. We write this pamphlet particularly for active trade unionists, co-operators and socialists because they are the ones who will have to face these problems in their most naked form, as unemployment increases. Furthermore, we know that the only way we, the coloured workers, can achieve any measure of real economic and social stability, is if the English workers understand the real reason why we have to leave our homeland. We hope that this pamphlet will help to develop a set of arguments which may foil any reactionary propaganda that will try to divide the working class amongst themselves.

We believe that this is in keeping with the best traditions of the working class movement and its slogan 'united we stand, divided we fall.' Most of our arguments in this pamphlet could apply to all immigrants whether they are Irish, Polish, Hungarian or even Scottish or Welsh. But there is one difference in the coloured worker. He is so conspicuous because of his colour that it is far easier to use him as a scapegoat than the white immigrant, because the white immigrants usually do not reveal themselves until they speak. That is why we give this pamphlet the title 'Don't Blame the Blacks.'

WHY WE COME

No man likes to leave his country of origin and in particular no man likes to leave a tropical climate for a land of snow, fog and rain. We leave our homeland not from choice but because we are forced to do so by economic and social circumstances. All the sunshine in the world is of no use if you are hungry, cannot find employment and do not enjoy any social amenities.

To give some examples of the economic and social conditions which exist among the coloured workers in their own country we will deal specifically with the colony of Jamaica, which provides the largest proportion of coloured immigrants to Britain. Another point of interest about Jamaica is that the conditions there are far better than many other colonial territories.

Out of a population of approximately 1,600,000 there are not less than 180,000 unemployed in Jamaica. For every 100 persons gainfully employed there are 33 persons (over fifteen years of age) who want work but cannot find any. (From ' Freedom Now,' published by the People's Freedom Movement.)

If there was a similar proportion in Britain there would be over $5^1/_2$ million unemployed. Trade Unionists will visualize how difficult this would make the Trade Union fight for better conditions and higher wages.

For those lucky enough to have a job in Jamaica all is not milk and honey. Consider the following table of wages and average hours and compare it with the cost of living which will be explained below.

Occupation	*Wages*	*Average Hours*	
Postmen			
Grade A	127/6d	54 hrs.	per week
" B	105/-	54 hrs.	
" C	105/-	54 hrs.	
Police			
Grade 1	£380 p.a.	70 hrs.	per week
" 2	£340 p.a.	70 hrs.	
Agricultural Workers			
A1 Male	9/6 per day	8 hrs. per day	
Female	7/6 "	8 " "	
A Male	8/6 "	8 " "	
Female	6/3 "	8 " "	
Bus Operators			
Skilled	60/-	48 hrs.	per week
Unskilled	30/-	48 hrs.	
Telephone Workers			
Skilled	172/9d.	45 hrs.	per week
Unskilled	65/11d.	51 hrs.	
Cigar and Cigarette Workers			
Skilled	63/10d.	42.8 hrs.	per week
Unskilled	51/6d.	53.5 hrs.	

The above list of wages and hours were extracted from the 1956 report on Jamaica (Published by H.M. Stationery Office).

The cost of living in Jamaica is one of the highest in the world. Numerous Jamaicans who have emigrated to the U.S.A. and Britain confirm that it is cheaper to live there than in Jamaica. In 1955 it cost $3\frac{1}{4}$ times what it cost to live in 1939. Adjusting the figures for comparison with wages, the cost of living in 1955 was $2\frac{1}{7}$ times what it was in 1942. What you could buy for £1 in 1942 now costs £2 21/10s. according to the Government Cost of Living index. But the real increase in the cost of living is much greater than this, as every Jamaican housewife knows.

In Jamaica there are no old age pensions, no unemployment pay, no family allowances. With the lack of such social amenities it is no wonder that the unemployed find it impossible to exist. Therefore, as soon as they can raise the money, they emigrate to a land which, they are told by constant propaganda, may solve their problems.

These deplorable conditions are not caused by accident, but are deliberately created by the ruling class, in order that they may maintain their system of exploitation.

DO WE CAUSE UNEMPLOYMENT?

The propaganda that coloured people cause unemployment is completely dishonest and is without any foundation. It wouldn't merit a reply but for the fact that the reactionary organisations who churn it out are quite conscious of what they hope to attain.

The ruling class has never failed to utilise any situation that they think will cause confusion amongst the working class in an attempt to divorce their thinking from the true cause of unemployment. One thing they tend to forget is the fact that in the 1929-31 slump in Britain there were over three million unemployed, and at that time the coloured population in Britain was negligible.

If we examine the situation thoroughly from a very simple economic point of view, we will realise that instead of the coloured worker causing unemployment, he has helped to create jobs. We must, after all, wear clothes, eat and live somewhere. Someone has to produce the things to satisfy his needs, thereby providing employment for the producers.

The true reason for unemployment is the Capitalist system of production and distribution. A study of history has shown that there was always unemployment under capitalism, which arises basically through the inability of the working class to buy back the goods that they produce.

The increasing trend toward mass unemployment is caused by the economic policy of the present Tory Government.

That is the true meaning of the credit squeeze, the Cohen Report and the cuts in government expenditure.

The capitalist class is helpless in the grip of the coming slump. There are already some six million unemployed in the United States, and by the winter of 1958-9 there will probably be anything up to two million jobless in Britain.

In such time of crisis, the workers naturally look for a way out of their difficulties. They become more readily responsive to a socialist explanation and a socialist solution to the problems presented by the slump.

At such times, the bosses do all in their power to sow the seeds of conflict among the workers. For they know that, united in the struggle and conscious of their own strength the workers could put paid to the rule of capital once and for all.

THREAT TO THE WORKING CLASS

It is always the policy of the ruling class to divide and conquer. The easiest way to achieve this is to have a scapegoat upon whom they can throw the blame for all the social ills, e.g., the Jews under Hitler.

The British ruling class is very skilful in this method, that is why we should not be surprised if this method is intensified in Britain.

Already Oswald Mosley (leader of the most reactionary fascists) and his gangs are re-organising themselves and the first type of propaganda they are using is that of colour discrimination. Again, if we look back on Germany before the war, we can see that the use of the Jews as scapegoats in Germany paved the way for Hitler. This is one of the methods used by the ruling class to maintain its hold.

If we examine the question of racial discrimination more thoroughly, we shall see that it not only drives a wedge between the coloured and white working classes but it also causes antagonism amongst the white workers themselves.

While the ruling class is preaching racial propaganda to white workers they are at the same time whispering into the coloured workers' ears that the cause of their difficulties is due to the fact that the white workers are against them, especially the more militant Trade Unionists. Of course, this type of propaganda can have a very nasty effect, for the simple reason that many of the trade unionists succumb to the reactionary propaganda, by showing a lack of tolerance and even at times show indifference when a coloured brother tries to become a member of their respective unions.

There is another dangerous feature which will develop — reactionary bodies which pose as organisations looking after the welfare of coloured people. These organisations are trying to revive the old order of having a number of domestic servants. They have already taken the first step by encouraging coloured women to take up such employment with the excuse that it is far better to work as a domestic servant than being on the dole. It might be correct if their intention was true, but if we look back into history we can see that this method of having a whole chain of cheap domestic labour will only enhance the ruling class power. It will intensify the exploitation of the women of Britain, and will cause the white working class to look upon the coloured women as befitted for no other type of employment, as the propagandists hope may happen.

The reactionaries have gone so far as to try to use coloured workers as a means of damping down the struggle among the English working class by importing coloured labour to work in jobs where the wages are low, and a man's social life is disrupted by the awkward shift system. Luckily the coloured workers refuse to be used as tools, as the latest London bus strike has shown. There was not a single coloured blackleg.

This colour discrimination can lead to direct conflict among the workers which we have noticed has actually started in the dole queue at some of the Labour Exchanges.

THE THREAT TO THE WHITE WORKER IS NOT THE COLOURED WORKER, BUT THE REACTIONARY POLICY OF THE BRITISH RULING CLASS.

WHAT TO DO

The majority of coloured workers before coming to England trust the English worker, for in him lies the key to freedom for these coloured people. Of course, we realise that any struggle to gain such freedom can only be achieved by a joint struggle of the white workers and the coloured workers. Therefore the first thing we must try to put over to each other is the fact that our struggle is the same, providing we have to sell our labour for a living.

Biological difference has nothing to do with what a man needs to maintain a decent standard of life.

The reactionary propagandists will try and prove from their point of view that the coloured worker can never integrate with the white workers, because of cultural differences, and so on. To accept such an argument is just playing into the hands of the British ruling class. We can show them that as workers of the world we can unite! The way to do this is to help the coloured workers fight in their own country for a better standard of living. The English workers should join in the struggle because the colonial struggle is part of the whole working class struggle. The first and most elementary step is to ensure the unionisation of all the workers, white and coloured. The same gang of useless profiteers live off the labour of white and coloured workers alike, in Britain and in the Colonies.

The lie that is put forward is, that if the coloured people achieve a better standard of living, the English workers standard will fall. If we, the workers, examine this carefully we shall realise that if the coloured people's standard of life in their own country were raised, it would not only provide employment for the English workers, but it would lessen coloured immigration.

The English workers should help us in our battle for equal rights. In doing so, they will help the coloured workers to realise that they must not fall for the reactionary propaganda which is constantly being whispered in their ears.

We must remember that colour prejudice, like anti-semitism, is a weapon of class rule, and as such must find no support in the ranks of those whose task it is to establish a world that is free from want. It should be clear that to end race prejudice and the colour bar, which the ruling class use as their main weapon to divide the working class, the coloured and white workers must join in the common struggle against capitalism.

Under Socialism production is for use and not for profit. Under Socialism there will therefore be work for all, whatever the colour of their skins.

We hope that this pamphlet will help to create the basis for complete unity among the coloured and English working classes.

* * *

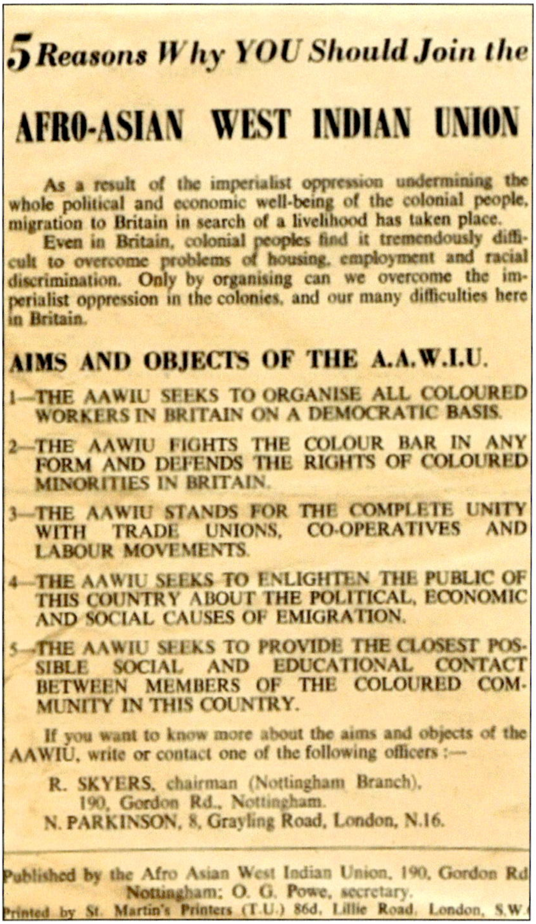

5 *Reasons Why YOU Should Join the*

AFRO-ASIAN WEST INDIAN UNION

As a result of the imperialist oppression undermining the whole political and economic well-being of the colonial people, migration to Britain in search of a livelihood has taken place.

Even in Britain, colonial peoples find it tremendously difficult to overcome problems of housing, employment and racial discrimination. Only by organising can we overcome the imperialist oppression in the colonies, and our many difficulties here in Britain.

AIMS AND OBJECTS OF THE A.A.W.I.U.

1—THE AAWIU SEEKS TO ORGANISE ALL COLOURED WORKERS IN BRITAIN ON A DEMOCRATIC BASIS.

2—THE AAWIU FIGHTS THE COLOUR BAR IN ANY FORM AND DEFENDS THE RIGHTS OF COLOURED MINORITIES IN BRITAIN.

3—THE AAWIU STANDS FOR THE COMPLETE UNITY WITH TRADE UNIONS, CO-OPERATIVES AND LABOUR MOVEMENTS.

4—THE AAWIU SEEKS TO ENLIGHTEN THE PUBLIC OF THIS COUNTRY ABOUT THE POLITICAL, ECONOMIC AND SOCIAL CAUSES OF EMIGRATION.

5—THE AAWIU SEEKS TO PROVIDE THE CLOSEST POSSIBLE SOCIAL AND EDUCATIONAL CONTACT BETWEEN MEMBERS OF THE COLOURED COMMUNITY IN THIS COUNTRY.

If you want to know more about the aims and objects of the AAWIU, write or contact one of the following officers :—

R. SKYERS, chairman (Nottingham Branch),
190, Gordon Rd., Nottingham.
N. PARKINSON, 8, Grayling Road, London, N.16.

Published by the Afro Asian West Indian Union, 190, Gordon Rd
Nottingham; O. G. Powe, secretary.
Printed by St. Martin's Printers (T.U.) 86d, Lillie Road, London, S.W.

Island Screams

Cara Thompson

Where are you from?
Nottingham.
No, like… where are you "from" from?
Oh. I see.
Well, that's easy.

I'm Windrush, hybrid, island spawn. I'm sun, I'm sea, I'm rain,
 I'm storm.
Cast out, cast in, I'm hope reborn and lost as soon as it was
 formed.
I'm bloody rivers, battleships, I'm ackee, saltfish, fish and chips,
I'm cocoa butter on your lips, I'm soursop, I'm apple pips.
I'm from the land of wooden huts, and bras made out of
 coconuts!
Where ganja burns and Europe tuts from inside of their history
 books.
I'm Blue Magic and hot-combed hair, I'm from the
 bloodstained windows where the ivory banks of Europe
 glare and leave my empty pockets bare,
I'm from a distant echoed threat, an island that I've never met,
Where sun and sea and blood and sweat are called your
 favourite vaycay yet!
From Caliban and animals, two steps away from Crusoe and
 his cannibals,
An island of Black Hannibals.
You dream about that package to Montego Bay you found on
 Thomson holidays

Where trees bend back and snap their roots to greet you on
your merry way
So many days of mine are spent repenting for a helpless crime,
I swing upon a slowly snapping vine and then I realise:
I'm sugar cane, I'm wind, I'm rain,
I'm hurricanes that tear the ground,
I'm ancestors that won't be found, whose bodies beat from
underground
I'm red skinned ghosts that haunt your dreams, I'm Nanny,
Seacole,
Pocomania screams that call across the sea and find their way
right back to me.

Does that answer your question?